Usborne
Sticker Dolly Dressing
Ballerinas

Leonie Pratt

Designed and illustrated by

Stella Baggott and **Vici Leyhane**

Contents

Meet the ballerinas

Nikki, Grace and Katy are three ballerinas who love dancing. They all went to the same ballet school and have been best friends ever since. They train with each other, dance in the same ballets and travel all over the world together.

This is Nikki. She's always wanted to be a ballerina. When she dances on stage, it really is a dream come true.

Sugarplum the cat

Katy is full of energy when she dances. She likes doing fast turns and big jumps across the stage.

Grace is just like her name – elegant and graceful. She adores thrilling audiences with powerful leaps and pirouettes.

The ballet mice

3

In the studio

Every day, the ballerinas go to the studio to train. Before they start dancing, they have to do lots of warm-up exercises to stretch their arms and legs.

Nikki and Katy are holding onto a wooden rail called a barre to help them balance.

Sleeping Beauty

The ballerinas are performing Sleeping Beauty. In this scene, Sleeping Beauty is about to prick her finger on a rose that she is holding. Grace is dancing the part of the Lilac Fairy and Nikki is the evil fairy, Carabosse.

costume fitting

The costumes that the ballerinas wear are made specially by the wardrobe mistress. Grace is dancing in a ballet called Giselle and needs to have the bodice of her costume fitted. Nikki and Katy have come along to see what other wonderful costumes the wardrobe mistress is making.

Cinderella

Katy is dancing the lead role in Cinderella. She has just danced down the stairs in a beautiful pink tutu. Grace and Nikki are the ugly sisters and are wearing bright dresses, big wigs and lots of make-up.

The Firebird

The Firebird is a ballet about a beautiful bird who lives in an enchanted garden. When a prince is in danger, the Firebird leaps to his rescue.

Coppélia

Nikki is pirouetting as if she is a mechanical doll on top of a music box. The dance is difficult, but she's done it so many times, she doesn't feel nervous at all.

The Nutcracker

The Nutcracker is a magical Christmas ballet about the adventures of a girl named Clara and her Nutcracker doll. The ballerinas are performing a scene where the Nutcracker and Clara follow the Sugarplum Fairy through the Land of Sweets.

In make-up

Ballerinas wear lots of make-up so that the audience can see their faces clearly when they're dancing. The ballerinas have their make-up done first of all, so that they don't get any on their costumes.

Once their make-up is finished, then they can start getting ready for their performance.

Coppélia

Swan Lake

Swan Lake is the ballet that Grace likes the best. She is dancing the part of Odette, the Swan princess. Nikki and Katie are also swans, and wear beautiful feather headdresses.

Shopping

Ballerinas dance on their tiptoes – this is called dancing on 'pointe'. This makes their legs look longer, but it means their ballet shoes wear out very quickly. The ballerinas buy their shoes at a special ballet shop that sells all kinds of beautiful things.

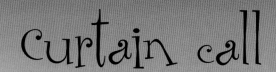

curtain call

It's the last night of a ballet tour and the ballerinas have come on stage to take the final bow. They feel so happy hearing everyone cheer and clap. The ballerinas have been given bouquets of flowers, and people in the audience are throwing roses onto the stage.

Picture album

The ballerinas have a special album where they keep pictures of all the ballets they have ever danced in. In these pictures, they're wearing the costumes for their latest ballet.

Sleeping Beauty

Sequins

Bows

Giselle

The Nutcracker

Buttons

Ribbon

Bows

Flowers

Cinderella

The Firebird

Coppélia

In make-up

COPPELIA

swan Lake

Nutcracker

Cinderella

Good Luck

Pages 16-17

Swan Lake

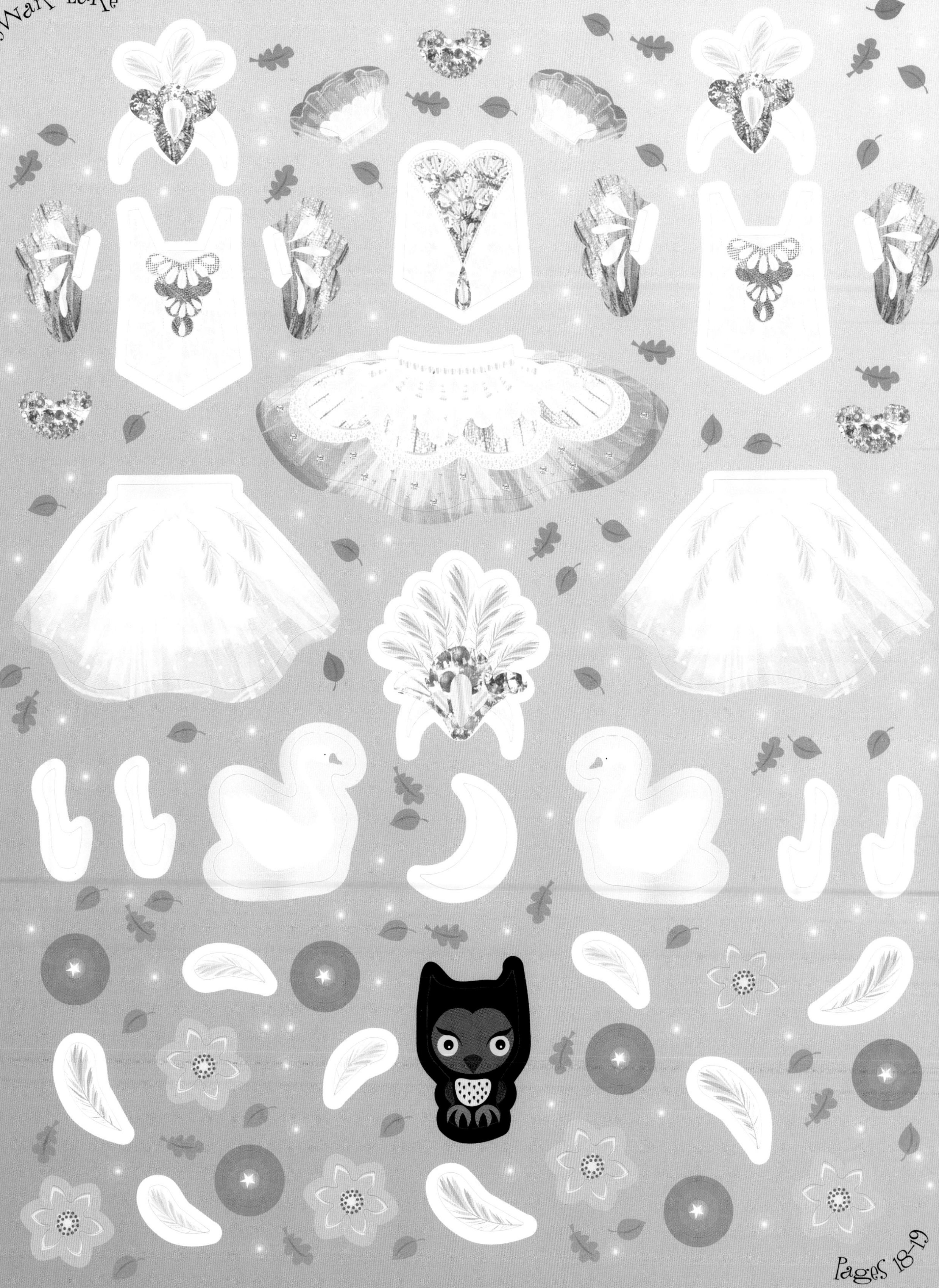

Pages 18-19

curtain call

Pages 22-23

Picture album

Nikki

Grace

Katy